Table of Contents

Table of Contents

Biography of Mann, Thomas (1875-1955)

Thomas Mann received the Nobel Prize for literature in 1929, and was the single most important prose writer of twentieth century Germany. Mann was born on July 6, 1875 to an upper middle class family in the seaport of Luebeck, Germany. After his father's premature death in 1891, the family fortune took a downturn, and they moved to Munich. When he graduated high school, Mann took a job as an insurance agent, but quickly grew to understand that literature was his passion. In Munich, Mann grew close to his mother, who was of Brazilian extraction, and she introduced him to a circle of intellectuals in the city. Mann moved to Italy in 1896 with his brother, Heinrich, to begin work on his first novel, *Buddenbrooks*.

The 1900 publication of *Buddenbrooks*, which traced the lives of a merchant family through several generations, made Mann rich and famous almost overnight. His only stab at drama, a 1905 prose piece called *Fiorenza*, met with less success. However, Mann cemented his reputation as a great writer with the publication of a number of short works, including *Tod in Venedig* (Death in Venice) in 1912. The novella describes the breakdown of an illustrious writer who travels to Venice and falls in love with a young Polish boy. The work was at least partially based on Mann's own experience, and much of his future work focused on the proximity between genius and madness and on the pull of homoeroticism.

Mann struggled with his homosexual tendencies in his literature and throughout his life, but married Katia Pringsheim, the daughter of a Jewish professor, in 1905. The author was deeply ambivalent about the typical bourgeois lifestyle he chose, but stayed with the decision to remain in a heterosexual marriage. With his wife, he had six children, three boys and three girls.

Mann continued to produce works of fiction, including the uncharacteristically satiric novel *Royal Highness* in 1916 and a shorter work titled *Early Sorrow* in 1929. In 1924, Mann finally published what many consider to be his greatest work, *The Magic Mountain*. The novel is set in a tuberculosis sanatorium in the Swiss Alps, a community that represents a microcosm of Europe directly before World War I. The protagonist, a healthy young man, comes to the sanatorium for a short visit, but ends up staying for seven years. Eventually, he finds fulfillment by leaving the community. The novel typifies the style that Mann is best known for: ironical, somber, and symbolic. Mann won the Nobel Prize for this novel, and for *Royal Highness*.

Between 1933 and 1943, Mann published a tetrology titled *Joseph and his Brothers*, on the history of the biblical character. In his famous *Doctor Faustus* (1947), Mann retold the famous myth as a composer who sells his soul to the devil in return for fame. Based on his friend, composer Arnold Schoenberg, the work expresses Mann's despair over German Nazism. Mann's last novels include *The Holy Sinner* (1951), *Confessions of Felix Krull*, and *Confidence Man* (1954).

Although Mann was not a political writer, he was forced to move on a number of occasions for political reasons. At the beginning of World War I, Mann conservatively believed in monarchy and German hegemony, but towards the end he was more inclined to side with France and the ideals of democracy. Mann left Hitler's Germany in 1933 and lived in France and Switzerland before settling in the United States in 1938. He taught at Princeton University in New Jersey for two years, but moved to Pacific Palisades, California to join an expatriate community of German intelligentsia including the composer Arnold Schoenberg, dramatist Berthold Brecht, and Mann's own brother, Heinrich. After World War II, during the McCarthy era, Mann grew disillusioned with American politics and moved back to Europe in 1952. He died in Zurich on August 12, 1955.

About Death in Venice

Although Mann is considered to be a deeply German writer, at the time that he began writing, Germany itself was fairly new to the world. When Death in Venice was published in 1912, a unified Germany had existed for a mere 41 years. Although Mann moved to Munich after high school, he was always aware of being North German and felt his more somber and serious artistic sense put him at odds with other artists in Munich. The connection between Germany and Italy in his work has clear political relevance, as the two countries unified their fragmented areas to become nations at similar points of time in history (King Victor Emmanuel began to rule over a unified Italy in 1861).

Mann wrote in the context of a number of literary styles. At the turn of the century, Naturalism reigned, and Mann sought to differentiate himself from writers such as Zola and Ibsen who faithfully transcribed even the most minute concrete details of daily life. In contrast to naturalist writers, Mann's precision is psychological, rather than physical. Specifically, Mann was influenced by other European masters including Tolstoy, whose epic sweep he admired, and Flaubert, whose labor over each and every sentence he emulated. Mann was also deeply indebted to the philosophy of Nietzsche, whose skeptical mode of analysis he adopted. Nietzsche claimed to be a great authority on the subject of decadence, and Mann's works focus almost exclusively on this topic, along with degeneracy and the decline of greatness.

The German Romantic composer, Richard Wagner, also significantly influenced Mann. Wagner pioneered the music-drama, in which the action of the drama takes precedence over the music itself. He popularized the leitmotif, a melodic fragment or phrase associated with a particular character or situation. The leitmotif carried over into literature in the form of a dominant, reoccurring theme, and Death in Venice is considered a primary example of its early use. The leitmotif of Death in Venice is death itself.

The issue of homosexuality in this novella negatively affected its reception. The issue was timely, as many great artists of the period including Gide, Wilde, and Rimbaud, were struggling with homosexuality. Mann's own diaries demonstrate his homosexual tendencies, despite his marriage. Homosexuality was not a widely accepted practice in early twentieth century Europe, and Mann neither attacks it nor praises it. Rather, he represents it as a symptom of the unhealthily obsessive nature of an artist. The irony about Mann's love story is that neither participant ever speaks to the other. Thus, Death in Venice must remain a homosexual love story in the most theoretical sense possible.

Character List

von Aschenbach

The protagonist. A well-known writer who leads an ascetic lifestyle and is taken by a whim to travel to Venice, where he falls in love with Tadzio.

travel agent

A British man and the only person in Venice honest with von Aschenbach regarding the threat of cholera.

Tadzio

A young Polish boy vacationing with his family in Venice with whom von Aschenbach falls in love.

barber

The hairdresser who changes von Aschenbach's appearance in an effort to make him look younger.

stranger in the cemetery

A tourist with a strange appearance whom von Aschenbach sees and considers following in Munich.

Jasiu

A Polish boy who is friends with Tadzio.

sisters

Tadzio's sisters, between the ages of fifteen and seventeen, whom von Aschenbach thinks look like nuns.

governess

The woman in charge of caring for Tadzio and his sisters.

mother

Tadzio's mother, a genteel looking Polish woman.

Major Themes

decadence/degeneracy

The theme of decadence was extremely popular in fin-de-siecle European literature. In addition, the degeneracy of the individual and society at large was represented in the works of Mann's contemporaries, including Oscar Wilde and Andre Gide. In Death in Venice, the issue of decadence appears through von Aschenbach's homoerotic feelings for the Polish boy, Tadzio. Although the feeling's spring from a reasonable source (the boy's beauty), von Aschenbach is decadent in how excessively fervent is feelings are, and his obsession leads to his downfall. Thus, decadence is closely related to, and indeed often causes, degeneracy.

the death's head

A death's head is a human skull or a more subtle representation of death. The death's head is the dominant leitmotif in this novella, with different representations of the same ominous man appearing in closer and closer proximity to von Aschenbach. First, while in the graveyard, he spots a strange foreigner who bares his teeth ferociously. Next, the frightening gondolier in Venice (who steers a boat that reminds von Aschenbach of a coffin) shares many of the same characteristics as the teeth-baring stranger, including a distinctive hat, reddish hair, and prominent teeth. The gondolier is physically closer to von Aschenbach than the stranger had been, but is still unavailable for conversation. The final appearance of the death's head occurs symbolically in von Aschenbach's hotel garden in the form of a singer. The singer again has similar characteristics to the other two symbolic men, including red hair and an important hat, and he pays special attention to von Aschenbach.

susceptibility to the environment

In response to Freud's writings, a psychological thrust occurred in literature with a focus on an examination of the human self in response to its environment. Von Aschenbach, as a sensitive artist, is especially susceptible to his environment. Von Aschenbach's moods are closely tied to the weather, and he decides to leave his first vacation spot in search of another merely because the weather and atmosphere do not suit him. Other characters are also responsive to the weather, and it is the general consensus in Venice that the unpleasant air is due to an excessively oppressive sirocco, rather than anything related to health concerns.

the Platonic ideal

Upon seeing Tadzio for the first time, Von Aschenbach's believes the boy exemplifes perfect beauty, is immediately relate him to the Greek ideal of beauty. Von Aschenbach uses the Greek image to abstract the boy's beauty and feel comfortable in his admiration. Thus, the Platonic ideal indicates that sexual love can exist as a precursor to a higher spiritual love that lacks physicality, a common practice between older men and younger boys. Von Aschenbach imagines himself as one of the great Greek masters, teaching Tadzio, whom he casts in the role of a young pupil. However, the writer fails to achieve the Platonic ideal, largely because he never speaks to Tadzio -- discourse is crucial to the Platonic ideal. Thus, von Aschenbach falls into a more lust-based appraisal of the boy.

costume/disguise

A large part of being an artist, whether literary or visual, is a preoccupation with the appearance of things. Costuming and artificiality strike von Aschenbach immediately, whether negatively or positively. On the ship to Venice, von Aschenbach immediately notices a group of young men and sees an older man who, by wearing a certain type of clothing and even putting makeup on his face, is attempting to appear young. Despite von Aschenbach's disgust at this old young man's vanity, the writer makes similar changes to his appearance only a few weeks later in the hopes of attracting Tadzio's attention. In addition, von Aschenbach admires the intentionality of Tadzio's costuming, specifically his sailor suit with a red bow for the beach, and his little peacoat with brass buttons for the city. Von Aschenbach tries to assimilate the little boy's costuming to his own by adding colorful bits to his clothing. In these attempts, von Aschenbach has lost good taste to the point where he even allows the barber to try to disguise him as a younger man by dying his hair and rouging his cheeks. In his new disguise, von Aschenbach appears uncomfortably similar to the man he scorned on his way to Venice.

Dionysus

Mann focused on degeneracy in his work, and is famously quoted as stating that during the twentieth century, Western civilization would fall as civilized men fell prety to their "Dionysian urges." Dionysus, also known as Bacchus, is the Greek god of drunkenness and hedonism, and was usually depicted as a drunken half-man half-goat surrounded by dancing half-naked youths. His lower half consisting of a goat's body refers to his unrepressed sexual desire. Von Aschenbach's final dream/vision before his death is a markedly Dionysian orgy, and the arrival of the "strangergod" is Dionysus himself, who was based on earlier gods in the Eastern tradition (hence the "stranger").

exoticism

As indicated by its title, Death in Venice consists partially of travel writing from Venice. The world holds three levels of familiarity for von Aschenbach. He is most at home in Munich and Germany, but has ceased to feel stimulated artistically, thus he looks to the exotic to refresh himself. Moving south of Germany to Italy, von Aschenbach is still in familiar territory (he has been here before, he is still in Europe) but the scene is less familiar, and quickly becomes menacing. The unfamiliarity of Italy makes Venice seem a "labyrinth," and the unhealthiness of the air is blamed on the "sirocco," a distinctly Mediterranean phenomenon.

An even more important, though more insidious representation of the exotic occurs in Mann's treatment of India. Although von Aschenbach never thinks of traveling to India, India is the substance of his first travel fantasy ("a crouching tiger gleam out of the knotty canes of a bamboo thicket") and is the most concrete source of his death (the cholera virus). If Italy is exotic and menacing to the German writer, India is even more so, and traces of the European fear of and fascination with the exotic East is evident in this work.

Glossary of Terms

cabana
a small hut on a beach used as a bathhouse

cipher
a symbol or key

collude
to conspire, become part of a confederacy

consummate (adj.)
extraordinary

cupola
a small dome-like lookout set on a roof

debauch
to corrupt morally

degeneracy
corrupt behavior, especially refering to sexual deviance

germicide
a chemical to kill germs

gesticulate
to gesture wildly

gondola
a lightweight boat used to travel through the canals in Venice

gondolier
a man who paddles a gondola

imminent
coming immediately

ineluctable
inevitable

loden
a coarse woollen fabric

lucidity
clarity

nebulous
unclear, misty

pellucid
transparent

perverse
cranky, perverted

quarantine
a period of time during which a person, house, or entire city is isolated because it is believed to carry contagious disease

retraction
a notice in a newspaper stating previously reported information was false

rouge
blush, makeup

sirocco
a hot and humid south or southeast wind that blows through Italy

sobriety
the opposite of intoxication

tootle
lowbrow music

vaporetto
a motorboat for transporting people along the canals in Venice

Short Summary

Von Aschenbach, born in Silesia to a civil servant and his Bohemian blooded wife, is a well-known writer. He was married for a short time before his wife died and now lives alone in Munich. After an unsatisfactory morning of work, he sets out on a walk and notices a strange looking tourist in a cemetery. Suddenly, von Aschenbach has a desire to travel. He briefly considers following the tourist, but instead takes the tram home.

Von Aschenbach lives an extremely ascetic life, dashing cold water on himself in the morning so that he can wake up and work on his writing. He has no close personal relationships. As a young boy, he was sickly, and has thus lived most of his life in this type of solitude. His literary work has brought him great fame. Usually, he portrays the stories of stoic heroes who appear noble, but are degenerate on the inside.

Two weeks after spotting the strange tourist in Munich, von Aschenbach embarks on a trip. He orders that his house in the German countryside be readied for his return in one month's time. He takes a train to Trieste, then boards a boat to a resort on an island in the Adriatic. Although he enjoys the trip, he is not completely satisfied, and decides to move on to Venice. On the boat, he meets an older man wearing makeup and rouge in an attempt to appear younger and socialize with a group of younger men. Von Aschenbach is disgusted by the man in makeup. When he arrives in Venice, von Aschenbach gets a free gondola ride because the gondolier is unlicensed and shoves off the pier before von Aschenbach has the chance to pay him.

At dinner at the hotel that night, von Aschenbach notices a Polish family of three girls and a beautiful boy of about fourteen, accompanied by a governess. The writer is struck by the boy's beauty. The next morning, he watches the boy, Tadzio, play with a friend on the beach, and then returns to his hotel room to inspect his own wrinkled face and gray hair. Von Aschenbach goes to Venice that afternoon and the oppressive humidity causes him to suffers a feverish attack. With ambivalence, von Aschenbach decides to leave Venice permanently, and tries to catch a train the next day. Unfortunately, his luggage is mislaid. He returns to the hotel, and feels joyful because while staying near Venice he can watch Tadzio, a truth that causes him slight discomfort.

When von Aschenbach's luggage is returned two days later, he unpacks and resolves to stay. Von Aschenbach quickly falls into a routine of watching Tadzio and using his inspiration to write. Walking behind him on the beach one morning, von Aschenbach almost overtakes him and tries to speak to him, but restrains himself. One evening, he runs into Tadzio unexpectedly and cannot control his surprised and excited facial expressions. Tadzio smiles back, aware of his own attractiveness. Von Aschenbach hurries away, and later whispers "I love you," a phrase obviously meant for the boy but only spoken after Tadzio has left.

During his fourth week at the hotel near Venice, von Aschenbach notices that many of the other guests are leaving. He hears rumors of a disease sweeping the city and tries to obtain concrete information about the outbreak. Von Aschenbach realizes that there is a fairly serious problem, but resolves not to leave. Anyone he asks reassures him that the smell of germicide in the city is merely evidence of the police being overly cautious. Von Aschenbach begins to follows Tadzio more actively, tailing the Polish family in Venice and watching the boy at a street musician concert in the hotel garden.

Von Aschenbach begins to alter his appearance to look younger. He adds colorful touches to his clothing, dyes and curls his hair, and wears rouge. All of these actions are behaviors he found despicable when he observed them in a fellow traveler earlier in the novel Although Tadzio realizes von Aschenbach is following him, he does not tell his family. In analyzing his relationship with Tadzio, Von Aschenbach imagines himself as Socrates and Tadzio as Phaedrus, thus fantasizing a relationship that mirrors the Greek Platonic ideal. In a half-awake dream, von Aschenberg predicts he will soon die, and that Tadzio, whom the writer assumes is at the resort because he is sickly, will die soon thereafter. Von Aschenbach witnesses a few of Tadzio's friends roughing him up on the beach. Tadzio walks away and looks back at von Aschenbach, knowing that he is watching. When von Aschenberg finally dies, most likely from cholera, the world is stunned to hear of the death of such a famous man.

Summary and Analysis of Chapter One

Summary:

The novel opens by introducing the great writer, Gustav Aschenbach, known since his fiftieth birthday as von Aschenbach. Von Aschenbach sets out on a solitary walk from his apartment in Munich and ruminates on his morning's work. It is early May, and as he passes through the Englischer Garten, he notices the weather is finally beginning to clear up. Von Aschenbach looks for a tram station at the North Cemetery, and when he is unable to find one, focuses his attention on the Byzantine building nearby. He notices a figure in the portico, evidently a foreign tourist, grimacing into the sunlight. The figure is wearing a bast hat, and notices von Aschenbach observing him. Upon being discovered, the writer walks away in embarrassment.

After noticing the tourist, von Aschenbach is struck with a sudden desire to travel, and imagines tropical scenes with lush vegetation. Previously, he had regarded tourism as merely an occasional diversion good for his health. Now that he is growing old and fears his artistic powers are faltering, he feels a sudden need to travel and escape from the duty of writing.

Von Aschenbach had experienced writer's block that very morning and felt that, although his work is still well received by the public, it lacks the sparkle of his younger work. He feels his usual summer alone in the German countryside will not cure him, because he finds the environment as oppressive as the city. Von Aschenbach locates the tram station, and considers turning back to find the tourist, but can no longer see him.

Analysis:

The passivity of the novella is established in this opening chapter. Mann specializes in psychodrama-his characters are not as concerned with interrelating as they are with their own mental processes. In the novella, the protagonist speaks to only few other individuals, and performs no action except walking and observing. However, in this first chapter, von Aschenbach commits to a course of action crucial to his life. Even passing through the streets of Munich is an aberration from his daily routine, and is thus a precursor to his even more unprecedented trip abroad. The stranger in the cemetery is highly important, both in sparking von Aschenbach's interest in travel and in hinting at the protagonist's homoerotic tendencies. In observing the tourist, von Aschenbach is not necessarily attracted to the man, but rather wishes to personify the mysterious stranger by undertaking his own travels.

The opening chapter establishes von Aschenbach as an important personage in society and simultaneously begins to undermine him. First, the prefix "von" to the protagonist's last name demonstrates that he has achieved aristocratic status. In addition, Mann's slightly over-wrought language invites the reader to take von Aschenbach as seriously as he takes himself; thus explaining the task of writing is extremely difficult, prestigious, and worthwhile.

Although, at first glance, the novel seems to be written in the third person, it is truly written in indirect style, or what the Germans term erlebte Rede. In other words, although the narrator writes about von Aschenbach in the third person, the reader can occasionally, and with increasing frequency as the novella progresses, drop into von Aschenbach's head to hear his thoughts. This style creates a double perspective and the possibility for dramatic irony, a literary device in which the reader knows more than the character. As the novella progresses, von Aschenbach spirals out of control, and the reader, privy to his thoughts, is partly dragged along, but also maintains enough distance to wonder whether his demise is really necessary.

Summary and Analysis of Chapter Two

Summary:

In this chapter, the nature of von Aschenbach's work is revealed. He has written an epic biographical novel of Frederick the Great, entitled *Maya*, and a novella entitled *The Wretched Figure*, which explores morality through a protagonist that justifies his own depravity by encouraging his wife to commit adultery. An essay entitled *Art and the Intellect* added to his fame, and is described as equivalent in worth to Schiller's essay work. Von Aschenbach was born in Silesia to a civil servant and his sensual Bohemian wife, whose ancestry lent a foreign appearance to the writer's face. Currently, he answers fan mail from all over the world.

Early in his life, von Aschenbach disciplined himself to become an artist. He grew up in solitude because he was too sickly to attend school, and his motto is "persevere." In his youth, his goal was to live to an old age and continue to produce great literature. To achieve this despite his illness-prone body, he knew he needed great discipline. Von Aschenbach wakes early each morning by dashing cold water on his face, and devotes his productive mornings to writing. He embodies the hero characters in his work: a somewhat passive, but ascetic intellectual. Von Aschenbach writes about the heroism of the weak, a self-possessed exterior hiding a dissolute interior, which is well suited to his times. As he grows older, his prose grows more stiff and formulaic and begins to be quoted as exemplary in official German textbooks.

Von Aschenbach married quite young, but his wife died soon thereafter. In this chapter, he is described as medium in height, dark, and with a large head on which he wears gold spectacles. His mouth is large and his eyes tired. Although he may live an ascetic existence, the subjects of his writings seem to ravage his face as if he were living through them.

Analysis:

This chapter interrupts the narrative style of the previous chapter to provide a biographical sketch of the author. His story closely parallels Mann's own history and artistic work. The somber father and mother with more artistic blood are a direct reference to Mann's civil servant father and his mother with Brazilian heritage. It soon becomes clear that von Aschenbach's personal life has been minimal to non-existent, making the nature of his artistic life extra-important in describing a personality the reader does not yet know well. In comparing von Aschenbach to the great German aesthetic theorist, Friedrich von Schiller, Mann clearly demonstrates his literary worth.

Writing in the tradition of French symbolists such as Flaubert, even Mann's smallest details hold heavy significance. In an anecdote about von Aschenbach's falling ill around his thirty-fifth birthday, a friend comments the writer has always lived "like this," clenches his fist, and has not been able to live "like this," and he unclenches his fist. This chapter also demonstrates that von Aschenbach is not born to constant industry, but forces himself to it, behavior that began at a very young age. In fact, this is an unnatural state, and is thus impossible to sustain. The last three chapters of the novella thus demonstrate how von Aschenbach behaves when he finally begins to live in an unclenched manner.

Rather than simply serving as a literary background to the rest of the novel, this chapter functions as a premature obituary in a novella that the reader knows will end in a death, due to the title. Because it functions as an obituary, in discussing von Aschenbach's life up to this point, the chapter is an omen for death.

Summary and Analysis of Chapter Three

Summary:

Two weeks later, von Aschenbach is ready to leave Munich, and asks that his house in the German countryside be prepared for his arrival four weeks hence. He takes a train to Trieste, Italy, where he boards a ship for Pola. He stops at a resort on an island in the Adriatic, populated mainly by Austrian tourists. Von Aschenbach is dissatisfied with the location, decides he is in the wrong place, and boards a ship to Venice.

The ship employee who sells von Aschenbach his ticket attempts to impress him with tidbits about how wonderful Venice is, which annoys von Aschenbach. He enters the ship somewhat disgusted, and as he watches the second-class passengers board, he notices a group of young men joined by an older man wearing rouge and dressed gaudily to appear younger. Von Aschenbach finds this man's obvious attempts at recapturing his lost youth revolting. Later, he lunches in the hold of the ship, and again observes the same group of men. When the coastline comes into view, the young men on the ship celebrate, but their older companion has become pitifully drunk.

As the ship enters Venice, von Aschenbach recognizes several landmarks. He puts his luggage into a gondola, and the rouged man drunkenly wishes him a pleasant stay. Von Aschenbach reflects on how like a coffin a gondola is, and realizes that the gondolier is not taking him to his requested destination, the pier. The gondolier explains that the pier will not accept luggage, and refuses the writer's request to turn back. A gondola holding musicians passes, and von Aschenbach gives them money. When von Aschenbach's gondola arrives at a landing stage, he disembarks, and the gondolier disappears before von Aschenbach can pay him. A nearby old beggar explains that he is the only unlicensed gondolier in Venice, and didn't want to be caught by the municipal officials on the pier.

Von Aschenbach is expected at his hotel and is greeted with respect. He takes a cup of tea on the terrace and then goes for a walk. Later in the day, he arrives for dinner too early and takes the chance to observe the other guests in the lobby. He notices that all nationalities are represented, but a Polish family consisting of three girls, ages fifteen to seventeen, and a beautiful boy of about fourteen accompanied by a governess, particularly interests him. Once in the dining room, he notices the boy's classically Greek symmetrical beauty. The girls are dressed severely and appear nun-like, while the boy has long curling hair and is clearly the favorite of the family. The children are dining with their mother, and when they leave after their meal, the boy glances back at Von Aschenbach.

The next morning, the weather is still quite gray. Von Aschenbach finds himself depressed and considers leaving Venice. At breakfast, he notes that the beautiful boy is allowed to sleep well into the morning while his sisters are awake very early. Later in the morning, he sees the boy wading in the ocean and admires his beautiful legs. On the beach, the boy leads a group of about ten children. By listening to the children playing, von Aschenbach discovers that the boy is named is Tadzio, and that his closest friend is Jasiu.

At noon, von Aschenbach returns to his room and studies his old face and gray hair in the mirror. During lunch, he gets a closer look at Tadzio and notices his teeth do not look well, meaning he is most likely sickly. That afternoon, von Aschenbach goes to Venice to take a walk, and feels feverish as a result of the crowd and sirocco. He realizes the pollution of the city makes him sick, and decides to travel to a different location. The next morning, von Aschenbach tries to leave. At breakfast, when he sees Tadzio, he almost changes his mind, but decides to continue his course. However, Von Aschenbach's luggage is put on the wrong train, forcing him to stay in Venice at least temporarily. Von Aschenbach finds himself surprisingly happy upon learning of this setback, and returns to the hotel. However, upon admitting that the reason for his happiness is Tadzio's presence, he despairs.

Analysis:

Here, Mann begins to rely increasingly on the literary technique of leitmotif. Various details are subtly repeated to create meaning. Von Aschenbach's discomfort on the boat to Venice is made clear by the reoccurrence of sordid details concerning the trip. The boat is grubby, the water is filthy, and his fellow passengers smell strange and are badly behaved. Mann splices these details in with other aspects of von Aschenbach's consciousness, making the section appear less like an intentional indictment of the voyage.

The most ominous section of this chapter is when von Aschenbach 's is unable to control his gondolier. Von Aschenbach immediately notes that the gondola feels like a coffin, an allusion to death, and then cannot control where his gondolier takes him. This encounter subtly echoes his encounter with the stranger in the Munich graveyard, another clear symbol of death. The gondolier and the graveyard stranger are strikingly similar, as they both have red hair and prominent teeth: the graveyard stranger bares his teeth in a strange grimace, and the gondolier shows his teeth with the effort of rowing. In addition, both men have specific hats. The stranger's is made of bast, and the gondolier's is a, "shapeless straw hat beginning to unravel." The unraveling hat perhaps symbolizes the onset of chaos in von Aschenbach's otherwise highly ascetic existence. Clearly, the graveyard stranger and the gondolier are highly similar, a repetition that illustrates destiny, not coincidence, has brought von Aschenbach to Venice.

Summary and Analysis of Chapter Four

Summary:

After two days, von Aschenbach's luggage is returned to him at the hotel and he unpacks completely, determined to stay in Venice. He falls into a routine of seeing Tadzio regularly, especially during mornings at the beach. He has accepted his attraction to Tadzio, but to reconcile his feelings, imagines an Ancient Greek scene of Socrates instructing Phaedrus, casting himself as Socrates, and Tadzio as Phaedrus. Von Aschenbach writes well when spying on Tadzio, although afterwards he feels exhausted and self-reproachful, as though he has done something base. However, he reasons that his readers will never know nor care from where his inspiration springs.

One morning, he follows the boy along the beach, and almost overtakes him. Von Aschenbach is tempted to speak to Tadzio, but stops himself at the last moment and immediately fears that someone has witnessed his intention. Von Aschenbach goes to bed early because he knows the possibility of seeing Tadzio after nine is slim. As time passes, Tadzio begins to return von Aschenbach's attention, walking past his table and looking at him on the way to his family's cabana. Von Aschenbach becomes so accustomed to his routine of watching Tadzio, that he is put off when Tadzio fails to appear on the beach one morning. Later on he discovers that Tadzio's family had gone to the city. He is caught off guard when he runs into Tadzio that night, and smiles in surprise and happiness. Tadzio smiles back, looking like Narcissus. Von Aschenbach is shaken by this image and hurries away to collect himself. Seated on a hotel bench, although he knows it is absurd, he murmurs "I love you."

Analysis:

This chapter is riddled with references to Ancient Greece. For more information about the Platonic concepts in this chapter, see the essay on Platonic love. As soon as von Aschenbach sets eyes on Tadzio, he associates him with, "Greek statuary of the noblest period." He begins to describe the boy as "beauty itself" and "form as the thought of God." Despite von Aschenbach's attempts to ennoble his love for Tadzio by putting it in the context of Greek philosophy, his reliance on the ideal of Platonic love is disingenuous. A prerequisite of the ideal relationship between a man and boy is that the man be the boy's mentor. Von Aschenbach is unable to speak to Tadzio, much less become his mentor.

The boy's attitude is also antithetical to the practice of Platonic love. The meaningful smile that he gives von Aschenbach is described as "the smile of Narcissus." Narcissus, in Greek mythology, is a beautiful young boy in love with his own image. He stares at his own reflection in a pool until he dies and is reborn as a flower. Significantly, the myth holds that the boy refused all offers of love. Thus, consummation of von Aschenbach's love seems highly unlikely.

This chapter presents von Aschenbach's true internal struggle: he realizes that he is in love with the boy, but works to assimilate these feelings into his normal philosophy, which proves unsuccessful. Thomas Mann was steeped in the philosophy of Nietzsche, who divides the Apollonian from the Dionysian. The former refers to form, order, and clarity, while the latter refers to abandon, joy, and debauchery. The categories are named after the Greek gods Apollo and Dionysus. Chapters One and Two demonstrate von Aschenbach's strong adherence to an Apollonian lifestyle. His day was a rigidly scheduled and ordered affair, and his artistic work was beginning to demonstrate this stiff lifestyle, as his prose grew overly structured and inflexible. However, von Aschenbach's dreams and his obsession with Tadzio, spliced into the writer's existence, demonstrate his tendency toward the Dionysian.

The last lines of this chapter are the climax of the novel. Up to this point, von Aschenbach has struggled to repress his feelings for Tadzio, but his final interaction with the boy demonstrates the triumph of the Dionysian forces in his mind. Finally, von Aschenbach verbally admits his love for Tadzio, although he mutters "I love you" alone, rather than in Tadzio's presence.

Summary and Analysis of Chapter Five

Summary:

During his fourth week at the Lido, von Aschenbach notices something is amiss. The number of guests at the hotel is falling rapidly, and there are no other German guests. The barber mentions offhand that he is staying on despite "the disease," but then refuses to define the disease. Von Aschenbach goes downtown immediately, and identifies the smell of germicide in the air. The city is plastered with posters warning against eating seafood. He asks a shopkeeper about the smell, and the man dismisses it, saying that it is a precautionary matter mainly of the police's concern.

At the hotel, von Aschenbach looks for news, but cannot find anything but vague warnings and reassurances. He feels that Venice is hushing up a dirty secret akin to his own secret of loving Tadzio, and is also concerned that Tadzio might leave to flee the epidemic. He follows the boy more regularly, even to a mass in Venice. He tails the Polish family around the city, follows them in a gondola, and is upset when he thinks they have noticed him. He justifies his obsession with the idea that it was the fashion in Ancient Greece for older men to love younger boys.

Von Aschenbach continues to search through German-language newspapers, which report an epidemic and criticize the Italian government for trying to hush it up, but also report retractions making the scale of the problem hard to measure. Von Aschenbach confronts the manager of the hotel about the plans to disinfect Venice, and considers the manager a hypocrite when he claims germicide is only a precaution.

Von Aschenbach attends a street singer performance in the front garden of the hotel. Although the music is sentimental and of poor quality, von Aschenbach enjoys it, as passion tends to debase artistic sensibilities. Tadzio is there, but guarded by his governess and mother, who have begun to notice von Aschenbach's attentions. When the singer comes around to collect money, von Aschenbach asks him why Venice is being disinfected, and the singer denies there is a disease. The singers perform a final song that has the audience laughing, but von Aschenbach remains somber. When he notices that Tadzio has also remained somber, von Aschenbach wonders despairingly if the boy is reacting to his own facial expressions. Von Aschenbach sits up at his table long after Tadzio and the other guests go to bed.

The next day, von Aschenbach goes to a British travel agency, where a travel agent finally tells him the truth. He says that a fatal Indian cholera had first moved east to China, west to Afghanistan and as far north as Moscow. It moved along trade routes, showing up in some Mediterranean cities including Palermo and Naples. In mid-May it hit Venice, but the cases were kept secret by the government, for fear of disturbing tourism. The travel agent urges von Aschenbach to leave Venice immediately.

Von Aschenbach imagines warning Tadzio's mother, although he has never spoken to her, but decides to collude in the secret and say nothing. He has a bad dream that night, filled with fear and desire as he watches a savage crowd dance and howl to the music of a flute, and joins them in worship of what he terms the "strangergod." He wakes up unnerved, and sees that most guests have fled the hotel. However, the Polish family remains, and von Aschenbach imagines everyone else might die so he can be left with Tadzio.

Von Aschenbach wishes to please Tadzio, and therefore begins to add colorful touches to his clothing. Next, he goes to the barber, who dyes his hair black, curls it, plucks his eyebrows, and adds makeup (rouge) to his face, to make him appear younger. Von Aschenbach is pleased, but confused. A storm wind begins to blow and the air turns humid. Von Aschenbach feels feverish.

He trails Tadzio around Venice, and although the boy looks back and realizes what von Aschenbach is doing, he does not tell his family. When he loses track of the Polish family, von Aschenbach buys and eats some overripe strawberries and finds himself in the same square in which he had decided to leave Venice a few weeks earlier. He sinks down on the steps of a well in the middle of the square, and dreamily talks aloud to Phaedrus, a cipher for Tadzio. He argues that although artists try to renounce the abyss of moral degeneracy, they are still drawn to it. He concludes that he will go and "Phaedrus" will remain, and when "Phaedrus" no longer sees him, then he will go too.

A few days later, von Aschenbach leaves his hotel to go for a walk and suffers from dizzy spells. He sees a large amount of luggage in the hotel lobby, and asks who is leaving, although he already seems to know the answer. He learns that the Polish family is leaving after lunch. He sees Tadzio playing with his friends, who are stronger than he is, but less beautiful. Jasiu defeats his friend in a wrestling match, driving his head hard into the sand. Von Aschenbach is about to rescue him when the other boys stop Jasiu. Tadzio walks away, and looks back at von Aschenbach, who sets out to follow him. Minutes later, people rush to the aid of von Aschenbach, who has slumped in his chair. That same day, the world learns of the famous writer's death.

Analysis:

In the final chapter of a tragedy, inevitability catches up with the protagonist. The gap of dramatic irony between the reader and the protagonist is closed somewhat, as von Aschenbach accepts certain facts he had been denying. Von Aschenbach begins to be more honest with himself about his false Platonic ideal, and begins to pursue Tadzio as an idol. Moreover, he becomes the rouge wearing older man in search of youth that he so despised on the boat trip to Venice, when he changes his appearance to please Tadzio.

The representation of Venice, which has been uneasy throughout the novella, takes a decided turn for the more sordid. Von Aschenbach describes it as a labyrinth, the presence of the water making it a mysterious and somewhat sick place. Of course, the city is literally sickened by the onset of the cholera epidemic, and von Aschenbach's earlier description of it as a "tourist trap" rings true. If the Venetian authorities were honest about the medical state of the city, a quarantine would be imposed and von Aschenbach would not be able to leave anyway. Ultimately, Venice traps von Aschenbach, becoming the city where the famous man buys overripe strawberries, contracts cholera, and dies.

The leitmotif of the sinister stranger appears for a final time in this chapter. The street singer who performs at von Aschenbach's hotel is reminiscent of the stranger in the graveyard and the gondolier. The singer also wears a specific hat, has large Adam's apple, and reddish hair. This death's head or Grim Reaper figure has become increasingly ominous throughout the chapters, as he moves physically closer to von Aschenbach and is available for more extensive conversation. The street singer is accompanied by the smell of carbolic acid, a germicide that foreshadows von Aschenbach's death.

The British travel agent's realistic description of the spread of the disease pins down the vague sense that fate is out to get von Aschenbach. The description of the Ganges Delta resonates exactly with von Aschenbach's original dream in Chapter One of a dense and dangerous jungle. He is destined not only to die in Venice, but to die of this exotic, tropical disease. By reading backwards, this original dream finally takes its proper significance.

The ending is slightly anti-climactic. In three short sentences, Thomas Mann brings us out of the claustrophobic world of the hotel in Venice, and widens the scope to the entire world. Von Aschenbach's personal history is finished, and the secret of his moral degeneration dies with him. Strangely enough, his public history remains unchanged, despite his experiences in Venice. His artistic reputation remains unharmed, and the world mourns the loss of a great author, and no more.

Summary and Analysis of Chapter Five

Suggested Essay Questions

1. Does von Aschenbach's relationship with Tadzio live up to the Platonic ideal? How does the boy's knowledge of his own attractiveness affect your evaluation?
2. In what ways does von Aschenbach exemplify the model of heroism that he writes about? Examine the pieces of work that Chapter Two claims he has written.
3. What is the role of fate in this novella? Does Mann's repetition of certain details (name them) indicate that von Aschenbach's death is inevitable? If not, how might von Aschenbach have avoided death?
4. What was the major factor in von Aschenbach's death--psychology or physicality? In a highly psychological novella such as this, is it believable that he succumbed to an actual virus, or was his moral corruption necessary to his death?
5. Perform a close reading of von Aschenbach's final dream/hallucination. Does he feel part of the savagery of the mob or does he hold himself aloof? Who is the "strangergod"?
6. In what way is this novella a microcosm of Europe pre-WWI? Does the travel agent represent a British perspective? What is Mann's stereotype concerning Italians? Is racism visible in this text?
7. Examine the changing descriptions of Venice as von Aschenbach moves from excitement at being there to feeling oppressed by the city. To what extent do the narrator's descriptions rely on the protagonist's feelings?
8. Does Mann view the artistic profession as inherently corrupt? Is von Aschenbach culpable for his own moral degeneration?
9. At the end of the novella, the world's opinion of von Aschenbach is unchanged, and the public will still react remember him based on his literary accomplishments as laid out in Chapter Two. Because all of the action in this novel occurs in his mind, has von Aschenbach done nothing wrong? Should the public's opinion of him remain unchanged? Is von Aschenbach correct in assuming that the reading public will not and should not know what inspired his great literature?
10. Analyze Mann's use of the free indirect style (a narrator who remains seperate from the protagonist but still has access to his thoughts). How does this add to the novella's ambivalence and ambiguities?

Platonic Love: What von Aschenbach had in mind

In order to more fully appreciate Mann's Death in Venice, the reader must understand the philosophical underpinnings of the text. Like Mann himself, von Aschenbach is a very well-read, well-educated man. The reader is privy to his thoughts, which often contain allusions to Ancient Greek philosophy the author is familiar with. As soon as von Aschenbach sees the boy, he begins to think of him in terms of a Greek ideal. The primary use of Greek philosophy in this text is von Aschenbach's effort to use Platonic philosophy to explain and justify his attraction to Tadzio, thus attempting to seperate his feelings from pure lust.

In Plato's philosophy, everything has a true form, a perfect representation of an idea. Earthly versions of this perfect form are imperfect reflections of the idea. For example, a horse can never exemplify the idea of "horseness" at its most perfect. The object of life and learning is to realize that the objects that we see around us are imperfect, and to transcend to a higher view of the world that is less material (i.e. to perceive "horseness" as a concept, rather than as a physical horse).

Therefore, by claiming that Tadzio is a representation of an ideal (von Aschenbach calls him "form as the thought of God"), the writer can view his attraction to the boy as a noble pursuit. By watching the boy, whom he supposedly perceives as the concept of perfect boyhood, rather than an attractive flesh and blood creature, von Aschenbach thinks he will be able to ascend to a higher level of Platonic understanding.

The specific text that von Aschenbach refers to is a dialogue (philosophical treatise) by Plato entitled *Phaedrus*. In the dialogue, Plato imagines Socrates and a beautiful boy named Phaedrus sitting under a tree discussing what the most ideal form of love. They conclude that love is necessary for mankind, and the most pure love can only exist between a man and a boy.

This idealization of male-male love was common in Ancient Greek society. In fact, it was not until the Middle Ages that Christians began to romanticize male-female relationships. Most men carried on heterosexual relationships and had families, but were also involved in less permanent homosexual relationships. The men were not defined as heterosexual, bisexual, or homosexual at that time, because the full spectrum of sexuality was more normalized and accepted than it has been for most of modern history. One reason male-male relationships were idealized is that they held no practical reproductive purpose; thus the men could focus on true love rather than the practical matters of reproduction.

Platonic Love: What von Aschenbach had in mind

Author of ClassicNote and Sources

Rachel Nolan, author of ClassicNote. Completed on April 01, 2006, copyright held by GradeSaver.

Updated and revised Adam Kissel April 20, 2006. Copyright held by GradeSaver.

Thomas Mann. Sketch of My Life. New York: Knopf, 1960.

Thomas Mann, tr. Michael Henry Heim. Death in Venice. New York: HarperCollins, 2004.

Donald A. Prater. Thomas Mann: A Life. Oxford; New York: Oxford University Press, 1995.

Marcel Reich-Ranicki. Thomas Mann and his Family. London: Collins, 1989.

Ed. Herbert Lehnerd and Eva Wessell. A Companion to the Works of Thomas Mann. Rochester, New York: Camden House, 2004.

Gerhard P. Knapp. "The Literary Encyclopedia." 2004-01-29. 2006-03-30. <http://www.litencyc.com/php/stopics.php?rec=true&UID=1355>.

Essay: The Artist's Struggle in the Work of Thomas Mann

by Anonymous
April 01, 2005

In his works "Tonio KrÃ¶ger," "Death in Venice," and "Tristan," Thomas Mann discusses the artist's struggle in terms of who he is, who he should be, and who he will be. In the three works, the artistic protagonists struggle with either a metaphorical or physical sickness, stemming mainly from their inability to reconcile the two polarities with which every artist struggles. Attempting to overcome these "sicknesses," the artists react to their problems differently, and in each of their reactions one can see Mann's assertion of what can become of an artist. In order to overcome his difficulty, Tonio KrÃ¶ger attempts to face his problems head-on, thereby moving towards eliminating them. Gustave von Aschenbach, however, runs from his metaphoric sickness to its polar opposite, which makes him even sicker. Finally, Deltev Spinell runs away from his issues, but towards nothing, which causes him to remain perpetually sick.

In all three works, the artist seeks to find a medium between the two polarities that drive him. Friedrich Nietzsche's theory on Greek tragedy influences Mann's view of this artist, who must aim to maintain balance between the Dionysian, or passionate and intoxicating forces, and the Apollonian, or the rational and detached forces. In "Tonio KrÃ¶ger," Mann portrays these clashing opposites through Tonio's parents-his southern, "dark, fiery mother" (78) and his northern, "reflective, puritanically correct" (131) father. Working as a writer in Munich, Tonio painfully tries to reconcile his "icy intellect and scorching sense" (92), and finds himself stuck as a "literary man" who stands removed from the world-only able to "label it and express it and discuss it and polish it off" (101). In order to face these influences of the Apollonian and reconcile them with his passion, Tonio decides to return to his childhood home.

Directly confronting his problems by returning to his northern roots, Tonio sees that he is neither entirely comfortable with the artists who call him "bourgeois" (104), or the bourgeois who almost arrest him. In fact, Tonio will never find himself amongst the fair-haired blue-eyed of the world, but as a passionate observer who can reconcile his opposing forces by seeking out his "bourgeois love of the human, the living and the usual" (131). Thus, Tonio realizes he may never find the perfect balance between the Dionysian and the Apollonian, or between his mother and father, but to apply both of these forces towards creating art, he can settle them in his work.

In "Death in Venice," Gustave von Aschenbach has similar difficulties balancing the Dionysian and Apollonian, for he is "painfully conscientious" (12), without even traces of the Dionysian. An utter perfectionist who champions will over nature,

Aschenbach's strictness with his art, in which his style is "fixed and exemplary" (14) is described as a malady-an inability to give into any indulgences and stray from his carefully plotted path. When Aschenbach visits Venice, he is no longer able to control his dormant Dionysian side, which takes over. He becomes reckless in his pursuit of Tadzio, and drinks contaminated water, eats possibly poisonous strawberries, and becomes the very image of death he had once condemned. Instead of balancing the Dionysian and Apollonian, Aschenbach runs away from the Apollonian-the aspect of himself he had known to this point, and behaves only passionately, rejecting any sort of balance between the two. Through Aschenbach's stay in Venice, which leads to his demise, Mann depicts the dangers of a heavy imbalance of the Dionysian and Apollonian.

In "Tristan," the writer Detlev Spinell surrounds himself with the sick, and claims to only reside at Einfried to have himself "electrified a bit," admitting he enjoys it there because "it is a feeling for style" (326-327). That Spinell remains in a house of sick when he is physically healthy is significant, as it shows that, like Aschenbach, he is detached and hides from the world-unable to enjoy life or embrace even a trace of the Dionysian. However, unlike Aschenbach who travels to Venice where he replaces the Apollonian with the Dionysian, by eliminating entirely his detached and intellectual side, Spinell runs away from the Apollonian but towards nothing. With Gabriele Klöterjahn's death, instead of having one passionate, highly emotional moment, Detlev Spinell "went away across the gravel...his gait was the hesitating gait of one who would disguise the fact that, inwardly, he is running away" (357). Without letting even a hint of the Dionysian into his life, Spinell is doomed to remain an invalid in Einfried forever, as he simply runs away from the Apollonian without rejecting it, but towards no balance with the Dionysian.

In all three works, Thomas Mann depicts detached observers whose inner struggles hinder their ability to fully live life, and all of whom travel somewhere to deal with these issues. Mann shows that the ultimate goal for these artists should be to balance out the Dionysian and Apollonian, like Tonio Kröger does, which would lead to a healthy life and fruitful career. Tonio Kröger, however, is the only one who is able to achieve this balance, as he alone confronts his difficulties, finding that the two polarities, which will always remain in conflict, can be reconciled by applying them and using them to create art. Gustave von Aschenbach and Detlev Spinell, however, run from their problems but towards no better solution, thereby causing them to remain "sick."

Essay: Art and Extremism

by Anonymous
April 02, 2005

In Thomas Mann's "Death in Venice," Gustave von Aschenbach is described as "the watcher" (73), who becomes interested in the young Tadzio, eventually leading to a dangerous obsession that causes his death. In the novella, Mann uses Aschenbach's sudden passionate fascination with the young Tadzio to portray the dangers of art taken to one extreme, and the need for a balance between the Dionysian and Apollonian-between drunken hedonism and detached rationalism. Aschenbach's heavy reliance on the Apollonian prior to his visit to Venice backfires on him, thrusting him to the Dionysian without any hope of finding stability. Tadzio's role in the story is passive, as he is the impetus for Aschenbach's transformation, but does not necessarily encourage Aschenbach's destructive behavior. Furthermore, Aschenbach himself is not fully aware of his changing, for he becomes somewhat delusional, dying relatively happily and peacefully.

Almost as soon as he sees Tadzio, Aschenbach becomes delusional, as discrepancies between what he perceives and what the narrator reveals become apparent. In Tadzio, Aschenbach sees a boy whose "face recalled the noblest moment of Greek sculpture-pale...the brow and nose descending in one line, the winning mouth, the expression of pure and godlike serenity" (25). However, "Tadzio's teeth were imperfect, rather jagged and bluish, without a healthy glaze of, and of that peculiar brittle transparency which the teeth of chlorotic people often show" (34). Interestingly enough, imperfect teeth, especially those with gaps, traditionally represent a lack of chastity-a far cry from Aschenbach's belief that Tadzio is "virginally pure and austere" (33).

As Aschenbach's obsession intensifies, he loses his grip on reality even further. In the beginning of the story, Aschenbach was "moved to shudder" when he looked at the "old man...with wrinkles and crow's feet round eyes and mouth; the dull carmine of the cheeks was rouge" (17). Later on, as the barber applies makeup to Aschenbach so that "a delicate carmine glowed on his cheeks...the dry, anaemic lips grew full, they turned the colour of ripe strawberries," Aschenbach "sat there comfortably; he was incapable of objecting to the process-rather as it went forward roused his hopes" (68). Aschenbach is unable to realize his sudden resemblance to this deathlike ominous figure, from his false-youth down to his red neck-tie.

The allusion to the ripe strawberries foreshadows Aschenbach's own consumption of the dangerous fruit in the next scene, and his inability to see his own downward spiral towards destruction. While following Tadzio, Aschenbach manages to "lose his bearing...he did not even know the points of the compass; all his care was not to lose sight of the figure after which his eyes thirsted" (69), and the strawberries become the quencher for his impulsive desire. Aschenbach grows more delusional, as Mann states that his sentences are "shaped in his disordered brain by the fantastic logic that governs our dreams" (70), and Aschenbach no longer lives in any sort of reality.

When a confused Aschenbach feels "a sense of futility and hopelessness," he is unsure "whether this referred to himself or to the outer world" (71). Since he is unsure of his situation, Aschenbach's death may be considered tragic to the reader, but not to Aschenbach himself, who "sat just as he had sat that time in the lobby of the hotel when first the twilit grey eyes had met his own" (73), and may not understand how his plunge into the world of the Dionysian ruined him. When Aschenbach dies, he simply "rested his head against the chair-back and followed the movements of the figure" (73), enjoying his last glimpse of Tadzio. Although he dies lonely, "a shocked and respectful world received the news of his decease" (73), and Mann indicates that his admirers will not soon forget him.

While Aschenbach of the novella dies without fully understanding the ramifications of his inability to balance the Dionysian and Apollonian, the Aschenbach of Luchino Visconti's dramatic film is aware of his problem and tragically sees that he cannot stop himself. In the film, Tadzio takes on a more active role, as he looks directly into the camera, luring Aschenbach by waiting for him to follow. The Tadzio of the film is seductive and beautiful not only in Aschenbach's eyes, but to the plain viewer. Thus, Aschenbach is no longer delusional, but is quite reasonable, since Tadzio engages in this game with him. Aschenbach is aware, then, of his precarious behavior, but sees no way to stop it. This is apparent in the scene near the close of the film, in which Aschenbach fervently pursues Tadzio, and when he loses him and sits by the well, is sweating and crying, as if to indicate his sadness at the inescapability of his fate. Perspiring and panting, Aschenbach appears urgent and pained, and does not seem to take pleasure in chasing Tadzio, but seems unable to stop himself.

By knowing his problem but being unable to control himself, Aschenbach is a more tragic figure, and his death is far unhappier than in the story. In the film's dramatic close, Mahler's music plays as Aschenbach gasps and appears injured, as black hair dye mixed with sweat drip down his face. He does not seem, as Mann described, to have a "relaxed and brooding expression of deep slumber," and though "the pale and lovely Summoner out there smiled at him and beckoned" (73), the film depicts Aschenbach being lured and painfully attempting to near Tadzio, as if pulled by a string, and somewhat unwillingly. Visconti ends the film by zooming out on the sad scene and does not close with Mann's somewhat uplifting message, in which the world mourns him. Instead, Aschenbach dies lonely and isolated, fully-knowing his problem and watching his descent into destruction, without the slightest ability to control it.

Essay: Art and Extremism

Quiz 1

1. **Venice is located on the**
   A. Mediterranean
   B. Black Sea
   C. North Sea
   D. Adriatic Sea

2. **At the beginning of Death in Venice, Aschenbach is living in**
   A. Berlin
   B. Munich
   C. Frankfurt
   D. Stuttgart

3. **In the North Cemetery, Aschenbach saw**
   A. Roman crosses
   B. many people
   C. Mortuary chapel in Moorish style
   D. none of the above

4. **In Gustave von Aschenbach's name, the "von" is**
   A. a letters-patent title
   B. both of the above
   C. an inherited title
   D. none of the above

5. **The name Aschenbach literally translated means**
   A. mound of ashes
   B. stream of ashes
   C. street of ashes
   D. lake of ashes

6. **A trait by which the "stranger in the cemetery" is described is "a sailor blouse with a red breast knot"**
   A. correct
   B. n/a
   C. n/a
   D. incorrect

7. **A trait by which the "stranger in the cemetery" is described is "obviously Bavarian"**
   A. correct
   B. n/a
   C. n/a
   D. incorrect

8. **The stranger in the cemetery suddenly causes Aschenbach to think about**
   A. travel
   B. both of the above
   C. youth
   D. none of the above

9. **Tadzio's mother portrays the same role as the stranger in the cemetery.**
   A. correct
   B. n/a
   C. n/a
   D. incorrect

10. **Jaschiu portrays the same role as the stranger in the cemetery.**
    A. correct
    B. n/a
    C. n/a
    D. incorrect

11. **The Venetian singer plays the same role as the stranger in the cemetery.**
    A. correct
    B. n/a
    C. n/a
    D. incorrect

12. **The young British man portrays the same role as the stranger in the cemetery.**
    A. correct
    B. n/a
    C. n/a
    D. incorrect

13. **The gondolier portrays the same role as the stranger in the cemetery.**
    A. correct
    B. n/a
    C. n/a
    D. incorrect

14. **Aschenbach's first dream/hallucination describes among other things bamboo thickets/crouching tigers, and marshlands/alluvial channels. The two geographical locations to which this dream refers are:**
    A. Europe/Africa
    B. Europe/Australia
    C. Africa/Asia
    D. Asia/Europe

15. **Aschenbach describes his mother as the daughter of a Bohemian musical conductor.**
    A. correct
    B. n/a
    C. n/a
    D. incorrect

16. **The description of Aschenbach's parents roughtly equates to those of Thomas Mann.**
    A. correct
    B. n/a
    C. n/a
    D. incorrect

17. **Aschenbach first decides to go to the island of**
    A. Cyprus
    B. Mallorca
    C. Pola
    D. Capri

18. **What is nonsensical when the boat cashier says to Aschenbach: "Delighted to serve you" and then, "Next."**
    A. The "next" has no money.
    B. The "next" is no one.
    C. The "next" has already paid.
    D. The "next" is the "false youth."

19. **Aschenbach's first gondola ride symbolizes his crossing the classical, mythological "Bridge of Tears."**
    A. correct
    B. n/a
    C. n/a
    D. incorrect

20. **The warm dry winds of the Mediterranean which bring death and disaster are called the "foehn" in this story.**
    A. correct
    B. n/a
    C. n/a
    D. incorrect

21. **The flowers in Aschenbach's room elicit yet another symbol of death. What does this room remind us of?**
    A. theater
    B. opera house
    C. concert hall
    D. none of these

22. **Tadzio's mother is most frequently referred to as the lady of**
    A. pearls
    B. jewels
    C. love
    D. tears

23. **Beach vendors sell sea shells, fruit, and cakes. Which of these, if any, has a direct relationship to the crux of the story?**
    A. sea shells
    B. cakes
    C. fruit
    D. none of these

24. **At one point, Aschenbach actually decides to leave Venice. His misdirected luggage allows/forces him to return.**
    A. correct
    B. n/a
    C. n/a
    D. incorrect

25. **Tadzio is described several times as "barefoot." Which other character is also so described?**
    A. sailor
    B. Jaschiu
    C. bathing master
    D. Aschenbach

Quiz 1 Answer Key

1. (**D**) Adriatic Sea
2. (**B**) Munich
3. (**D**) none of the above
4. (**A**) a letters-patent title
5. (**B**) stream of ashes
6. (**D**) incorrect
7. (**D**) incorrect
8. (**B**) both of the above
9. (**D**) incorrect
10. (**D**) incorrect
11. (**A**) correct
12. (**D**) incorrect
13. (**A**) correct
14. (**D**) Asia/Europe
15. (**A**) correct
16. (**A**) correct
17. (**C**) Pola
18. (**B**) The "next" is no one.
19. (**D**) incorrect
20. (**D**) incorrect
21. (**D**) none of these
22. (**A**) pearls
23. (**C**) fruit
24. (**A**) correct
25. (**C**) bathing master

Quiz 2

1. **While Aschenbach watches the strolling musical troupe on the hotel lawn, what symbolic drink does he consume?**
    A. red wine
    B. pineapple juice
    C. grapefruit juice
    D. none of these

2. **After the performance, Aschenbach gives the leader of the musical troupe a large, friendly handshake.**
    A. correct
    B. n/a
    C. n/a
    D. incorrect

3. **The plague spreading through Venice is**
    A. yellow fever
    B. typhus
    C. cholera
    D. Black Plague

4. **The river from whose delta the plague originates is the**
    A. Euphrates
    B. Nile
    C. Rhine
    D. Ganges

5. **The first two persons to die from the plague are the sailor (bargee) and Aschenbach.**
    A. correct
    B. n/a
    C. n/a
    D. incorrect

6. **Aschenbach's has a dream like an "orgy of death." In this dream, Aschenbach prepares to meet the**
    A. God
    B. life force
    C. devil
    D. stranger god

7. **The two "life force" figures in this work are the British travel agent and Tadzio.**
   A. correct
   B. n/a
   C. n/a
   D. incorrect

8. **The abandoned object on the beach, which allows the soul to be "freed," is a/an**
   A. camera
   B. empty beach chair
   C. empty glass
   D. abandoned piece of luggage

9. **The character described as "the Summoner" is Aschenbach.**
   A. correct
   B. n/a
   C. n/a
   D. incorrect

10. **Von Aschenbach imagines that the relationship between Socrates and Phaedrus is analagous to the teacher/pupil relationship between himself and Tadzio.**
    A. correct
    B. n/a
    C. n/a
    D. incorrect

11. **Von Aschenbach imagines that the relationship between Eros and Psyche is analagous to himself and Tadzio, who can only be united in death.**
    A. correct
    B. n/a
    C. n/a
    D. incorrect

12. **The relationship between Zephyr, Apollo and Hyancinthus is analagous to Aschenbach falling in love with himself.**
    A. correct
    B. n/a
    C. n/a
    D. incorrect

13. **"An excellent choice," he rattled on. "Ah, Venice! What a glorious city." Who said this?**
    A. ticket seller
    B. British travel agent
    C. Jaschiu
    D. Aschenbach

14. **"Give her our love, will you, the p-pretty little dear...Little sweety-sweety sweetheart" was said by**
    A. Tadzio
    B. bathing master
    C. Tadzio's mother
    D. false youth

15. **"I will pay nothing whatever if you do not take me where I want to go," was said by**
    A. gondolier
    B. Aschenbach
    C. old boatman
    D. false youth

16. **"The signore has had a ride for nothing," was said by**
    A. Phaedrus
    B. gondolier
    C. Aschenbach
    D. old boatman

17. **"He is sickly...He will most likely not live to grow old." The "He" in this statement is**
    A. Tadzio
    B. Jaschiu
    C. Phaedrus
    D. Critobolus

18. **"But _____ was a truly repulsive sight. He could not carry his wine like them. He was pitiably drunk."**
    A. gondolier
    B. Aschenbach
    C. old boatman
    D. false youth

19. "There behind a table sat a man with a beard like a goat's. He had his hat on the back of his head, a cigar stump in the corner of his mouth." This quote refers to
  A. sanitary inspector
  B. ticket seller
  C. Aschenbach
  D. false youth

20. "One of the party, in a dandified buff suit, a rakish panama with a colored scarf, and a red cravat, was loudest of the loud." This refers to
  A. baritone buffo
  B. Aschenbach
  C. Critobolus
  D. false youth

21. "It was the lovely boy...he was barefoot...it seemed he had never worn shoes," This quote refers to
  A. Dream II
  B. Dream IV
  C. Dream III
  D. Dream I

22. The mythological "River Styx" is symbolized by Aschenbach's trip to
  A. Trieste
  B. Lido
  C. Pola
  D. Como

23. Aschenbach refers to Tadzio as a "little Phaeax." Phaecia is a legendary land of mariners whose love of luxury was well known.
  A. correct
  B. n/a
  C. n/a
  D. incorrect

24. "If it were not that sea and beach were waiting for me, I should sit here as long as you do," Who said this?
  A. Tadzio
  B. Jaschiu
  C. Aschenbach
  D. Eros

25. **"Among the knotted joints of a bamboo thicket the eyes of a crouching tiger gleamed," is a description from**
   A. Dream II
   B. Dream IV
   C. Dream III
   D. Dream I

Quiz 2 Answer Key

1. **(D)** none of these
2. **(D)** incorrect
3. **(C)** cholera
4. **(D)** Ganges
5. **(D)** incorrect
6. **(D)** stranger god
7. **(D)** incorrect
8. **(A)** camera
9. **(D)** incorrect
10. **(A)** correct
11. **(A)** correct
12. **(D)** incorrect
13. **(A)** ticket seller
14. **(D)** false youth
15. **(B)** Aschenbach
16. **(D)** old boatman
17. **(A)** Tadzio
18. **(D)** false youth
19. **(B)** ticket seller
20. **(D)** false youth
21. **(C)** Dream III
22. **(B)** Lido
23. **(A)** correct
24. **(C)** Aschenbach
25. **(D)** Dream I

Quiz 3

1. **The barber does not perform the following to Aschenbach:**
   A. rouge his cheeks
   B. dye his hair black
   C. add a bow to his neck
   D. curl his hair

2. **Von Aschenbach has been to Venice before.**
   A. correct
   B. n/a
   C. n/a
   D. incorrect

3. **Jasiu is**
   A. von Aschenbach's first name
   B. Tadzio's friend
   C. Tadzio's father
   D. the stranger in the cemetary

4. **The Hotel de Bains in Venice is the**
   A. third resort von Aschenbach tries
   B. first resort von Aschenbach tries
   C. second resort von Aschenbach tries
   D. only resort von Aschenbach tries

5. **Von Aschenbach finally hears the truth about the epidemic from**
   A. Tadzio's mother
   B. a British travel agent
   C. the manager of the hotel
   D. the barber

6. **In Munich, von Aschenbach wakes himself up by**
   A. dashing cold water on himself
   B. setting an alarm
   C. having his mother remind him to get up
   D. hearing a rooster

7. **Von Aschenbach writes best in the**
  A. evening
  B. morning
  C. afternoon
  D. park

8. **Von Aschenbach has written a novel about the historical figure**
  A. Goethe
  B. Louis XIV
  C. Napoleon
  D. Frederick the Great

9. **Von Aschenbach usually spends his summers**
  A. in Venice
  B. in Munich
  C. on an island
  D. in the German countryside

10. **Von Aschenbach was born in**
  A. Berlin
  B. Munich
  C. Bavaria
  D. Silesia

11. **Von Aschenbach**
  A. lives with a homosexual partner in Munich
  B. has never been married
  C. has been married
  D. regularly has affairs with young boys

12. **Tadzio has how many sisters?**
  A. one
  B. two
  C. none
  D. three

13. **Tadzio's governess strikes von Aschenbach as**
    A. vulgar
    B. deformed
    C. beautiful
    D. evil

14. **As a boy, von Aschenbach was**
    A. sickly
    B. good at sports
    C. girlish
    D. not very literate

15. **Von Aschenbach favors what type of hero in his works?**
    A. able to perform magic
    B. extremely strong physically
    C. outwardly noble, inwardly degenerate
    D. outwardly degenerate, inwardly noble

16. **Von Aschenbach thinks his audience will know the inspiration for his writing was corrupt.**
    A. correct
    B. n/a
    C. n/a
    D. incorrect

17. **Von Aschenbach's "Wretched Figure"**
    A. steals
    B. has an affair with a boy
    C. commits murder
    D. encourages his wife to commit adultery

18. **Death in Venice was originally written in**
    A. German
    B. Italian
    C. Latin
    D. French

19. **Von Aschenbach is**
    A. a small man with a large head
    B. a large man with a small head
    C. Italian
    D. black

20. **Von Aschenbach's mother has**
    A. Italian blood
    B. English blood
    C. Bohemian blood
    D. Brazilian blood

21. **Von Aschenbach takes a train from Munich to**
    A. Venice
    B. Bavaria
    C. Silesia
    D. Trieste

22. **The primary mode of transport in Venice is**
    A. gondola
    B. car
    C. motorboat
    D. horse and carriage

23. **On board the ship to Venice, von Aschenbach is disgusted by**
    A. the lunch he is served
    B. the smell of germicide
    C. an old man dressed as a young man
    D. a dead animal

24. **Gondolas remind von Aschenbach of**
    A. trains
    B. his childhood
    C. coffins
    D. beds

25. **How does von Aschenbach catch the virus?**
   A. drinking canal water
   B. kissing Tadzio
   C. eating overripe strawberries
   D. eating dinner at the hotel

Quiz 3 Answer Key

1. **(C)** add a bow to his neck
2. **(A)** correct
3. **(B)** Tadzio's friend
4. **(C)** second resort von Aschenbach tries
5. **(B)** a British travel agent
6. **(A)** dashing cold water on himself
7. **(B)** morning
8. **(D)** Frederick the Great
9. **(D)** in the German countryside
10. **(D)** Silesia
11. **(C)** has been married
12. **(D)** three
13. **(A)** vulgar
14. **(A)** sickly
15. **(C)** outwardly noble, inwardly degenerate
16. **(D)** incorrect
17. **(D)** encourages his wife to commit adultery
18. **(A)** German
19. **(A)** a small man with a large head
20. **(C)** Bohemian blood
21. **(D)** Trieste
22. **(A)** gondola
23. **(C)** an old man dressed as a young man
24. **(C)** coffins
25. **(C)** eating overripe strawberries

Quiz 4

1. **Von Aschenbach's final dream hallucination involves**
   A. Tadzio
   B. canals
   C. gondolas
   D. a savage mob

2. **Just before von Aschenbach dies,**
   A. he goes swimming on the beach
   B. he declares his love to Tadzio
   C. Tadzio looks back at him
   D. he drinks a glass of wine

3. **When von Aschenbach is feeling unsettled, he usually**
   A. writes
   B. goes for a walk
   C. drinks wine
   D. talks to strangers

4. **When excited by the stranger in the cemetery, von Aschenbach identifies his feeling as**
   A. desire
   B. loathing
   C. fear
   D. wanderlust

5. **Mann compares von Aschenbach's essays to**
   A. Goethe's
   B. Schopenheuer's
   C. Schiller's
   D. Nietzche's

6. **Every day, von Aschenbach**
   A. writes a letter to his mother
   B. answers fan mail
   C. writes a letter to Tadzio
   D. writes a letter to his wife

7. **Von Aschenbach's face**
    A. looks youthful
    B. has extensive scarring
    C. has registered the emotions he writes about
    D. has a burn on the lip

8. **Von Aschenbach travels to Venice**
    A. with the Polish family
    B. in pursuit of the Polish family
    C. alone
    D. with his wife

9. **How long does von Aschenbach stay in Munich after seeing the stranger in the cemetery?**
    A. a month
    B. two weeks
    C. a day
    D. a week

10. **What does von Aschenbach consider to be Venice's main attributes?**
    A. "fairy-tale like" and "a tourist trap"
    B. "fairy-tale like" and "vibrant"
    C. "boring" and "too dry"
    D. "a tourist trap" and "too dry"

11. **What object falls while the rouged man from the boat talks to von Aschenbach?**
    A. his cane
    B. his eyes
    C. his toupe
    D. his dentures

12. **The gondolier refuses to take von Aschenbach where he wants to go because**
    A. the location is too far away
    B. he doesn't give a reason
    C. it does not take luggage
    D. he doesn't know where it is

13. **Tadzio's hair is**
    A. long and curly
    B. short and curly
    C. long and straight
    D. short and straight

14. **As Tadzio is bathing, the first feature of his body that von Aschenbach notices is his**
    A. neck
    B. legs
    C. arms
    D. torso

15. **What does von Aschenbach say at the end of Chapter Four?**
    A. "I need to get out of here"
    B. "I love you"
    C. "What is your name?"
    D. "I miss Munich"

16. **Who does he say this to?**
    A. Tadzio
    B. his wife
    C. Tadzio's mother
    D. no one

17. **Tadzio's voice is**
    A. he is mute
    B. low and loud
    C. high and weak
    D. low and quiet

18. **Von Aschenbach thinks Tadzio is**
    A. anemic
    B. prone to heart problems
    C. lame
    D. weak in the kidneys

19. **The only part of Tadzio's body von Aschenbach finds unattractive is his**
     A. ears
     B. nose
     C. legs
     D. teeth

20. **Von Aschenbach describes Tadzio's sisters as**
     A. brown-skinned
     B. nun-like
     C. ungainly
     D. attractive

21. **Von Aschenbach thinks exposure to sun tends to**
     A. sunburn
     B. corrupt
     C. increase the intellect
     D. have positive health benefits

22. **At the resort, von Aschenbach goes to bed early because**
     A. he is drunk
     B. there is no longer any chance of seeing Tadzio
     C. he is lonely
     D. he doesn't want to talk to his wife

23. **Von Aschenbach compares Tadzio's smile to that of**
     A. Schiller
     B. Socrates
     C. Narcissus
     D. Plato

24. **Mann writes that love and passion tend to**
     A. increase artistic ability
     B. decrease desire to produce art
     C. increase desire to produce art
     D. decrease artistic discernment

25. **Von Aschenbach dies**
    A. in his apartment
    B. in his hotel room
    C. on the beach
    D. in his house

Quiz 4 Answer Key

1. **(D)** a savage mob
2. **(C)** Tadzio looks back at him
3. **(B)** goes for a walk
4. **(D)** wanderlust
5. **(C)** Schiller's
6. **(B)** answers fan mail
7. **(C)** has registered the emotions he writes about
8. **(C)** alone
9. **(B)** two weeks
10. **(A)** "fairy-tale like" and "a tourist trap"
11. **(D)** his dentures
12. **(C)** it does not take luggage
13. **(A)** long and curly
14. **(B)** legs
15. **(B)** "I love you"
16. **(D)** no one
17. **(C)** high and weak
18. **(A)** anemic
19. **(D)** teeth
20. **(B)** nun-like
21. **(B)** corrupt
22. **(B)** there is no longer any chance of seeing Tadzio
23. **(C)** Narcissus
24. **(D)** decrease artistic discernment
25. **(C)** on the beach

ClassicNotes

GrⲀdeSaver™

Getting you the grade since 1999™

Other ClassicNotes from GradeSaver™

1984
Absalom, Absalom
Adam Bede
The Adventures of Augie March
The Adventures of Huckleberry Finn
The Adventures of Tom Sawyer
The Aeneid
Agamemnon
The Age of Innocence
The Alchemist (Coelho)
The Alchemist (Jonson)
Alice in Wonderland
All My Sons
All Quiet on the Western Front
All the King's Men
All the Pretty Horses
Allen Ginsberg's Poetry
The Ambassadors
American Beauty
And Then There Were None
Angela's Ashes
Animal Farm
Anna Karenina
Anthem
Antigone
Antony and Cleopatra
Aristotle's Ethics
Aristotle's Poetics
Aristotle's Politics
As I Lay Dying
As You Like It

Astrophil and Stella
Atlas Shrugged
Atonement
The Awakening
Babbitt
The Bacchae
Bartleby the Scrivener
The Bean Trees
The Bell Jar
Beloved
Benito Cereno
Beowulf
Bhagavad-Gita
Billy Budd
Black Boy
Bleak House
Bless Me, Ultima
Blindness
Blood Wedding
The Bloody Chamber
Bluest Eye
The Bonfire of the Vanities
The Book of the Duchess and Other Poems
The Book Thief
Brave New World
Breakfast at Tiffany's
Breakfast of Champions
The Brief Wondrous Life of Oscar Wao
The Brothers Karamazov
The Burning Plain and Other Stories
A Burnt-Out Case
By Night in Chile

Call of the Wild
Candide
The Canterbury Tales
Cat on a Hot Tin Roof
Cat's Cradle
Catch-22
The Catcher in the Rye
The Caucasian Chalk Circle
Charlotte Temple
Charlotte's Web
The Cherry Orchard
The Chocolate War
The Chosen
A Christmas Carol
Christopher Marlowe's Poems
Chronicle of a Death Foretold
Civil Disobedience
Civilization and Its Discontents
A Clockwork Orange
Coleridge's Poems
The Color of Water
The Color Purple
Comedy of Errors
Communist Manifesto
A Confederacy of Dunces
Confessions
Connecticut Yankee in King Arthur's Court
The Consolation of Philosophy
Coriolanus

For our full list of over 250 Study Guides, Quizzes,
Sample College Application Essays, Literature Essays and E-texts, visit:

www.gradesaver.com

ClassicNotes

GradeSaver™

Getting you the grade since 1999™

Other ClassicNotes from GradeSaver™

The Count of Monte Cristo
The Country Wife
Crime and Punishment
The Crucible
Cry, the Beloved Country
The Crying of Lot 49
The Curious Incident of the Dog in the Night-time
Cymbeline
Daisy Miller
David Copperfield
Death in Venice
Death of a Salesman
The Death of Ivan Ilych
Democracy in America
Devil in a Blue Dress
Dharma Bums
The Diary of a Young Girl by Anne Frank
Disgrace
Divine Comedy-I: Inferno
Do Androids Dream of Electric Sheep?
Doctor Faustus (Marlowe)
A Doll's House
Don Quixote Book I
Don Quixote Book II
Dora: An Analysis of a Case of Hysteria
Dr. Jekyll and Mr. Hyde
Dracula

Dubliners
East of Eden
Electra by Sophocles
The Electric Kool-Aid Acid Test
Emily Dickinson's Collected Poems
Emma
Ender's Game
Endgame
The English Patient
The Epic of Gilgamesh
Ethan Frome
The Eumenides
Everyman: Morality Play
Everything is Illuminated
The Faerie Queene
Fahrenheit 451
The Fall of the House of Usher
A Farewell to Arms
The Federalist Papers
Fences
Flags of Our Fathers
Flannery O'Connor's Stories
For Whom the Bell Tolls
The Fountainhead
Frankenstein
Franny and Zooey
The Giver
The Glass Castle
The Glass Menagerie
The God of Small Things
Goethe's Faust
The Good Earth

The Good Woman of Setzuan
The Grapes of Wrath
Great Expectations
The Great Gatsby
Grendel
The Guest
Gulliver's Travels
Hamlet
The Handmaid's Tale
Hard Times
Haroun and the Sea of Stories
Harry Potter and the Philosopher's Stone
Heart of Darkness
Hedda Gabler
Henry IV (Pirandello)
Henry IV Part 1
Henry IV Part 2
Henry V
Herzog
Hippolytus
The Hobbit
Homo Faber
House of Mirth
The House of the Seven Gables
The House of the Spirits
House on Mango Street
How the Garcia Girls Lost Their Accents
Howards End
A Hunger Artist
I Know Why the Caged Bird Sings

For our full list of over 250 Study Guides, Quizzes,
Sample College Application Essays, Literature Essays and E-texts, visit:

www.gradesaver.com

ClassicNotes

GradeSaver™

Getting you the grade since 1999™

Other ClassicNotes from GradeSaver™

I, Claudius
An Ideal Husband
Iliad
The Importance of Being
  Earnest
In Cold Blood
In Our Time
In the Time of the
  Butterflies
Inherit the Wind
An Inspector Calls
Interpreter of Maladies
Into the Wild
Invisible Man
The Island of Dr. Moreau
Jane Eyre
Jazz
The Jew of Malta
Joseph Andrews
The Joy Luck Club
Julius Caesar
The Jungle
Jungle of Cities
Kama Sutra
Kate Chopin's Short
  Stories
Kidnapped
King Lear
King Solomon's Mines
The Kite Runner
Last of the Mohicans
Leaves of Grass
The Legend of Sleepy
  Hollow
A Lesson Before Dying
Leviathan

Libation Bearers
Life is Beautiful
Life of Pi
Light In August
Like Water for Chocolate
The Lion, the Witch and
  the Wardrobe
Little Women
Lolita
Long Day's Journey Into
  Night
Look Back in Anger
Lord Jim
Lord of the Flies
The Lord of the Rings:
  The Fellowship of the
  Ring
The Lord of the Rings:
  The Return of the
  King
The Lord of the Rings:
  The Two Towers
A Lost Lady
The Lottery and Other
  Stories
Love in the Time of
  Cholera
The Love Song of J.
  Alfred Prufrock
The Lovely Bones
Lucy
Macbeth
Madame Bovary
Maggie: A Girl of the
  Streets and Other
  Stories

Manhattan Transfer
Mankind: Medieval
  Morality Plays
Mansfield Park
The Marrow of Tradition
The Master and
  Margarita
MAUS
The Mayor of
  Casterbridge
Measure for Measure
Medea
Merchant of Venice
Metamorphoses
The Metamorphosis
Middlemarch
A Midsummer Night's
  Dream
Moby Dick
A Modest Proposal and
  Other Satires
Moll Flanders
Mother Courage and Her
  Children
Mrs. Dalloway
Much Ado About
  Nothing
My Antonia
Mythology
The Namesake
Native Son
Nickel and Dimed: On
  (Not) Getting By in
  America
Night
Nine Stories

For our full list of over 250 Study Guides, Quizzes,
Sample College Application Essays, Literature Essays and E-texts, visit:

www.gradesaver.com

ClassicNotes

GradeSaver™

Getting you the grade since 1999™

Other ClassicNotes from GradeSaver™

No Exit
Northanger Abbey
Notes from Underground
O Pioneers
The Odyssey
Oedipus Rex or Oedipus the King
Of Mice and Men
The Old Man and the Sea
Oliver Twist
On Liberty
On the Road
One Day in the Life of Ivan Denisovich
One Flew Over the Cuckoo's Nest
One Hundred Years of Solitude
Oroonoko
Oryx and Crake
Othello
Our Town
The Outsiders
Pale Fire
Pamela: Or Virtue Rewarded
Paradise Lost
A Passage to India
The Pearl
Percy Shelley: Poems
Perfume: The Story of a Murderer
Persepolis: The Story of a Childhood
Persuasion
Phaedra

Phaedrus
The Piano Lesson
The Picture of Dorian Gray
Poe's Poetry
Poe's Short Stories
Poems of W.B. Yeats: The Rose
Poems of W.B. Yeats: The Tower
The Poems of William Blake
The Poetry of Robert Frost
The Poisonwood Bible
Pope's Poems and Prose
Portrait of the Artist as a Young Man
Pride and Prejudice
The Prince
The Professor's House
Prometheus Bound
Pudd'nhead Wilson
Pygmalion
Rabbit, Run
A Raisin in the Sun
The Real Life of Sebastian Knight
Rebecca
The Red Badge of Courage
The Remains of the Day
The Republic
Rhinoceros
Richard II
Richard III

The Rime of the Ancient Mariner
Rip Van Winkle and Other Stories
The Road
Robinson Crusoe
Roll of Thunder, Hear My Cry
Romeo and Juliet
A Room of One's Own
A Room With a View
A Rose For Emily and Other Short Stories
Rosencrantz and Guildenstern Are Dead
Salome
The Scarlet Letter
The Scarlet Pimpernel
The Seagull
Season of Migration to the North
Second Treatise of Government
The Secret Life of Bees
The Secret River
Secret Sharer
Sense and Sensibility
A Separate Peace
Shakespeare's Sonnets
Shantaram
Short Stories of Ernest Hemingway
Short Stories of F. Scott Fitzgerald
Siddhartha

For our full list of over 250 Study Guides, Quizzes,
Sample College Application Essays, Literature Essays and E-texts, visit:

www.gradesaver.com

ClassicNotes

GrIdeSaver™

Getting you the grade since 1999™

Other ClassicNotes from GradeSaver™

For our full list of over 250 Study Guides, Quizzes,
Sample College Application Essays, Literature Essays and E-texts, visit:

www.gradesaver.com

16276671R00045

Printed in Great Britain
by Amazon